Sports Illustrated KIDS

T0053120

Olympic
GOATs

The Greatest Athletes of All Time

BY BRUCE BERGLUND

CAPSTONE PRESS
a capstone imprint

Published by Capstone Press, an imprint of Capstone
1710 Roe Crest Drive, North Mankato, Minnesota 56003
capstonepub.com

Library of Congress Cataloging-in-Publication Data
Names: Berglund, Bruce R., author.
Title: Olympic GOATs : the greatest athletes of all time / by Bruce Berglund. Other titles: Olympic greatests of all time Description: North Mankato, Minnesota : Capstone Press, 2022. | Series: Sports illustrated kids. GOATs | Includes bibliographical references. | Audience: Ages 8-11 | Audience: Grades 4-6 |
Summary: "How do you pick Olympic GOATs? Is it gymnast Simone Biles or swimmer Michael Phelps? Or maybe it's the entire 1992 basketball team. With so many sports, how do you choose? It comes down to stats, history, and hunches. Read more about some of the legends of the Olympic Games and see if you agree that they're the greatest of all time"-- Provided by publisher.
Identifiers: LCCN 2021042756 (print) | LCCN 2021042757 (ebook) |
  ISBN 9781663976376 (hardcover) | ISBN 9781666321692 (paperback) |
  ISBN 9781666321708 (pdf) | ISBN 9781666321722 (kindle edition)
Subjects: LCSH: Olympic athletes--Biography--Juvenile literature. | Olympics--History--Juvenile literature.
Classification: LCC GV721.53 .B47 2022 (print) | LCC GV721.53 (ebook) | DDC 796.092/2--dc23
LC record available at https://lccn.loc.gov/2021042756
LC ebook record available at https://lccn.loc.gov/2021042757

Editorial Credits
Editor: Ericka Smith; Designer: Sarah Bennett; Media Researcher: Svetlana Zhurkin; Production Specialist: Katy LaVigne

Image Credits
Associated Press: 26, Jim Gerberich, 15, Natacha Pisarenko, 13; Library of Congress: 22; Newscom: picture-alliance/dpa/Peter Kneffel, 21, Reuters/Lucy Nicholson, 12, Sipa USA/GEPA pictures/Andreas Pranter, 11, Sipa USA/GEPA pictures/Andreas Pranter, 7; Shutterstock: A.Ricardo, 6, Apostle (star background), cover, back cover, and throughout, Iurii Osadchi, 8, 24, Leonard Zhukovsky, 17, 20, 28, magico110, 5 (bottom), Petr Toman, 10, photoyh, 5 (top), Sunward Art (star confetti), 4, 6, 8, 10, 12, 14, 16, 18, 20, 22, 24, 26, 28; Sports Illustrated: Al Tielemans, cover (top right and bottom right), Heinz Kluetmeier, cover (bottom middle), 9, 25, John Biever, 14, Manny Millan, cover (bottom left), 18, 19, 23, 27, Robert Beck, cover (top left), 16, Simon Bruty, cover (top middle)

All records and statistics in this book are current through the 2021 Tokyo Olympics.

Table of Contents

Olympic Heroes 4

Simone Biles 6

Eric Heiden 8

Usain Bolt 10

Lauryn Williams 12

Greg Louganis 14

Shaun White 16

The Dream Team 18

Yuna Kim 20

Jesse Owens 22

Miracle on Ice 24

Wilma Rudolph 26

Michael Phelps 28

Glossary 30

Read More 31

Internet Sites 31

Index 32

About the Author 32

Words in **bold** appear in the glossary.

Olympic Heroes

The Olympic Games first began more than 2,700 years ago in **ancient** Greece. Men from different cities competed every four years. They had sprinting races, long-distance runs, and boxing matches. The champions became famous across Greece.

Today, the Summer and Winter Olympics include hundreds of different events. There are still sprinting races and boxing matches. There are also newer sports like snowboarding and sport climbing. Now both men and women compete.

Athletes today **represent** different countries. Billions of people around the world watch the Olympics on TV. The greatest Olympic champions are famous not just in their home countries but also around the globe. People everywhere remember the greatest Olympians of all time. In some places, there are statues of the GOATs of the Olympic Games.

More than a billion people watched the opening ceremony of the 2008 Summer Olympics in Beijing, China.

Sonja Henie won three gold medals in figure skating. She became famous around the world and even starred in movies. This statue is in her hometown of Oslo, Norway.

Simone Biles

Olympians come in all sizes. Weightlifters are bulky. Cross-country skiers are thin. Volleyball players are tall. Figure skaters are short.

Gymnasts are some of the smallest Olympians. And the greatest gymnast is one of the smallest. Simone Biles stands 4 feet, 8 inches tall. That might be shorter than you.

Biles completing a balance beam routine during the 2016 Rio Games

Biles is small. But her feats in gymnastics are huge. Olympic sports like gymnastics have many different events. Women's gymnastics has six events, including individual and team events. At the 2016 Olympic Games in Rio de Janeiro, Brazil, Biles won gold in four of the six events. At the Tokyo Games in 2021, Biles and the U.S. team took silver in the women's all-around, and Biles earned bronze on the balance beam.

Biles has even invented new gymnastic moves, or skills. There are four moves named after Biles—more than any other gymnast.

Nadia Comaneci

Nadia Comaneci of Romania was the first gymnast to receive a perfect score of 10 in the Olympics. She won three gold medals at the 1976 Summer Olympics in Montreal, Canada.

Eric Heiden

At the 1980 Winter Olympics in Lake Placid, New York, American Eric Heiden won every event in speed skating. He skated the shortest race—the 500-meter sprint—in just about 38 seconds. He also won the longest race—the 10,000 meters. He had to skate more than six miles in about 14 minutes. Heiden also won the three races in between—the 1,000 meters, the 1,500 meters, and the 5,000 meters.

Heiden didn't just win—he set records in every event. It is very unusual for an athlete to win short races and long-distance races. But he was an amazing athlete.

Ireen Wüst

Ireen Wüst won more Olympic medals than any other speed skater. In four Winter Games, she won five gold medals, five silver medals, and one bronze medal—a total of 11 medals. She is the greatest Dutch athlete in Olympic history.

Heiden training for the 1980 Olympics at Lake Placid

Usain Bolt

At the Olympics in ancient Greece, the most popular event was the shortest sprint race. Athletes ran as fast as they could from one end of the stadium to the other, about as long as two football fields. The Olympic Games for that year were named in honor of the man who won the race.

We don't name the Olympics for a champion anymore. Instead, some people call the winner of the shortest sprinting race the "fastest man alive." The runner who won that title more than anyone else is Usain Bolt of Jamaica. Bolt won the 100-meter dash and the 200-meter dash in three straight Olympics.

Bolt also won two gold medals in the 4 x 100-meter relay race. At the 2012 London Olympics, Bolt and his three teammates set a world record.

How Fast Are Olympians?

Running

100-meter sprint

Florence Griffith-Joyner, 1988, 21.3 miles per hour (34.3 kilometers per hour)

Usain Bolt, 2012, 23.2 mph (37.3 kph)

Cycling

200-meter sprint

Becky James, Great Britain, 2016, 41.7 mph (67.1 kph)

Jason Kenny, Great Britain, 2016, 46.8 mph (75.3 kph)

Alpine Skiing (downhill)

Sofia Goggia, Italy, 2018, 62.6 mph (100.7 kph)

Aksel Lund Svindal, Norway, 2018, 64.7 mph (104.1 kph)

Luge (singles)

Tatjana Hüfner, Germany, 2010, 82.3 mph (132.4 kph)

Felix Loch, Germany, 2010, 94 mph (151.2 kph)

Tatjana Hüfner

Lauryn Williams

The first **modern** Summer Olympic Games were held in Athens, Greece, in 1896. The Winter Olympics began in 1924 in Chamonix, France. Since that time, 128 athletes have competed in both the Summer and Winter Olympics.

At the 2014 Winter Games in Sochi, Russia, Lauryn Williams made history. She became only the fifth athlete to win a medal at both the Winter and Summer Olympics. She was the first woman from the United States to do this.

Williams ran the last leg of the 4 x 100-meter relay during the 2012 London Olympics.

Williams started her Olympic career as a sprinter. She won silver in the 100-meter dash in the 2004 Athens Olympics. At the 2012 London Olympics, she won gold in the 4 x 100-meter **relay**. Then she switched to bobsledding. Bobsled teams need someone fast to push the sled at the start. That person also has to be strong. Williams worked out and built muscle to push the sled. With her teammate, she won silver in the two-woman bobsled race.

Williams pushes the sled as her teammate jumps into the front to steer the bobsled.

Greg Louganis

Olympic athletes in any sport can get hurt. Skiers crash. Skaters fall. Sprinters strain muscles.

American diver Greg Louganis had a scary injury at the 1988 Summer Olympics in Seoul, South Korea. Louganis jumped high off the diving board. He did a backward somersault and hit the back of his head on the board. Fans were shocked. People wondered if he could still compete.

Guo Jingjing

Guo Jingjing is one of the most successful women divers ever. She won four gold medals and two silver medals in three Summer Olympics. She is one of the most popular athletes in her home country of China. Jingjing and her husband were even **contestants** on the Chinese version of the TV show *The Amazing Race*. They won the race!

Louganis did finish the event. And he won. Louganis won gold in both diving events that year. He had already won two gold medals at the 1984 Summer Olympics in Los Angeles, California. He was the first man ever to sweep the diving events in two Olympics.

Before winning gold in 1984 and 1988 (shown below), Louganis won silver at the 1976 Summer Olympics—when he was only 16 years old.

Shaun White

The Olympics are always adding new sports. Snowboarding was added to the Winter Olympics in 1998. American Shaun White first competed in the snowboarding event in 2006. He was 19 years old. White had already won gold in snowboarding at the Winter X Games. At the Olympics, he became the first athlete to win gold in both the X Games and the Olympics.

White competing in the 2014 Olympic Games in Sochi, Russia

White is a great athlete. He has done moves that no other snowboarder has ever done. At the 2018 Winter Olympics, he won his third gold. He also received the highest score ever in halfpipe.

White is also a famous athlete. He has millions of followers on social media platforms.

Chloe Kim

Chloe Kim was 17 years old when she won gold in halfpipe at the 2018 Winter Olympics. Her parents had moved from South Korea to the United States before she was born. Because the 2018 Winter Games were held in South Korea, her grandmother was able to watch her compete in person for the first time.

The Dream Team

There are many team sports in the Olympics. They include soccer, volleyball, baseball, and hockey.

One of the greatest Olympic teams ever was the 1992 U.S. men's basketball team. They won gold at that year's Summer Games in Barcelona, Spain. Some say this was the greatest team to play together in any sport. They became known as the "Dream Team."

This was the first time professional players could compete in Olympic basketball. The Dream Team was made up of NBA stars. Eleven of them are in the Basketball Hall of Fame.

The Dream Team easily won its games. They helped make basketball popular around the world. Many NBA players from other countries said they decided to play basketball because of the Dream Team.

Charles Barkley was the top scorer for the Dream Team. He was the top scorer again for the U.S. team at the 1996 Olympics and won a second gold medal.

Michael Jordan won his second Olympic gold medal with the Dream Team. He also won at the 1984 Summer Games, when the U.S. Olympic basketball team was made up of the best college players.

Yuna Kim

Figure skaters start at a young age. Yuna Kim of South Korea began skating when she was only five years old. Right away, her coach saw she had talent. Kim competed in her first **international tournament** at age 11 and won.

For the next 11 years, Kim won a medal every time she competed. She was the first figure skater to finish every tournament on the medal **podium**. She was also the first women's figure skater to win every major world tournament, from junior competitions to the Olympics. She set a record at the 2010 Winter Olympics in Vancouver, Canada. She received the highest score ever in women's figure skating.

At the start of the Olympic Games, a giant cauldron is lit with the Olympic flame. It is a great honor to light the cauldron. Kim lit the cauldron at the 2018 Winter Olympics in South Korea.

Yuna Kim is a celebrity in South Korea. She has been on TV shows and in ads. She has even made songs with K-pop artists.

Tessa Virtue and Scott Moir

Canadians Tessa Virtue and Scott Moir have won more Olympic medals than any other figure skaters. They won three gold medals and two silver medals in ice dancing. They started skating together when Moir was nine years old and Virtue was seven years old.

Jesse Owens

American Jesse Owens made Olympic history when he participated in the Summer Games in 1936. He won gold medals in the 100-meter dash, the 200-meter dash, the long jump, and the 4 x 100-meter relay. He was the first athlete to win four gold medals in one Olympics.

Owens made history at the 1936 Summer Olympics (at right), but his greatest feat as an athlete was at a college track meet in 1935. He set three world records in three different events on the same day.

But Owens's feat was bigger than winning medals. The 1936 Olympics were held in Berlin, Germany. At that time, **Nazi** leader Adolf Hitler ruled Germany. Hitler and the Nazis said that white people were better than people who were not white. Owens showed the world that they were wrong.

When people list the greatest athletes ever, Owens's name is often near the top. He is also one of the most important athletes ever because he showed that the idea of **white supremacy** is wrong.

Carl Lewis

Carl Lewis matched Jesse Owens's record of four gold medals at the 1984 Olympics in Los Angeles. Like Owens, he won gold in the 100-meter dash, the 200-meter dash, the long jump, and the 4 x 100-meter relay. Lewis set a record by winning the long jump in four straight Olympics.

Miracle on Ice

Kids still know the famous speech by Coach Herb Brooks: "You were born to be hockey players—every one of you, and you were meant to be here tonight. This is your time. . . . Now go out there and take it."

In 1980, the Soviet Union's hockey team was the best in the world. They had won gold in four straight Olympics. In 1979, the Soviets had crushed a team of NHL all-stars.

The U.S. team was made up of college players. For months, Brooks trained the team for one goal. They needed to beat the Soviets. At the Lake Placid Olympics, the Americans stunned the world with a 4–3 win over the Soviets. Two days later, they won the gold medal. The U.S. hockey team's win over the Soviets is still remembered as the greatest underdog victory in Olympic history.

Hayley Wickenheiser

Hayley Wickenheiser is considered the greatest women's hockey player of all time. She led Canada to gold medals in four straight Olympics. She has the record for most goals in Olympic women's hockey.

The 1980 U.S. hockey team celebrates a win against the Soviet Union's hockey team.

Wilma Rudolph

When Wilma Rudolph was five years old, she had a bad disease called polio. The disease caused her to lose strength in her left leg. Rudolph wore a brace and received weekly treatments. The clinics in her hometown in Tennessee would not treat Black patients. Once a week, Rudolph and her mother had to travel 50 miles to a hospital that would treat her.

Rudolph was finally able to walk without a brace when she was 11 years old. She started running. And she was fast! Rudolph made the Olympic track team in 1956. She was only 16 years old. She won bronze in the 4 x 100-meter relay. In 1960, she won three gold medals at the Olympics in Rome, Italy.

Rudolph won gold in the 100-meter dash, the 200-meter dash, and the 4 x 100-meter relay at the Rome Olympics.

The 1960 Olympics were the first to be shown on TV in the United States and Europe. Rudolph became famous around the world. When she returned home, white leaders of her town wanted to have a parade in her honor. But they wanted it to be only for the town's white people. Rudolph said that she would be in the parade only if Black people were allowed to watch as well. So the white leaders decided to **integrate** the event.

Jackie Joyner-Kersee

American Jackie Joyner-Kersee also had to overcome health problems to become an Olympic athlete. She suffers from severe asthma, which affects breathing. Once, she had an asthma attack at a track meet and had to go to the hospital. Joyner-Kersee competed in track events in four different Olympics. She won a total of six medals, including three golds.

Michael Phelps

No Olympic athlete has won more medals than Michael Phelps. He first competed at the 2000 Summer Games in Sydney, Australia. He was 15 years old. His best finish was fifth place. In 2004, he started an Olympic winning streak. He won six gold medals and two bronze medals.

At the 2008 Summer Games in Beijing, Phelps broke the record for most gold medals in a single Olympics. In 1972, American swimmer Mark Spitz had won seven gold medals. Phelps tied the record when he won a race by the length of a finger. Underwater photographs had to prove that he had won. Phelps then won his eighth gold to set a new record.

Phelps competing in the 200-meter butterfly event during the 2016 Rio Olympics

Phelps won four more golds and two silvers at the 2012 Olympics. Then he retired from swimming races. But then he decided to train once more for the Olympics. At the 2016 Summer Olympics in Rio, Phelps won five more gold medals and a silver medal.

Greatest Olympic Champions

Most Gold Medals

Athlete	Country	Sport	Years	Medals
Michael Phelps	USA	swimming	2004–2016	23
Larisa Latynina	Soviet Union	gymnastics	1956–1964	9
Paavo Nurmi	Finland	track	1920–1928	9
Mark Spitz	USA	swimming	1968–1972	9
Carl Lewis	USA	track	1984–1996	9

Most Total Medals

Athlete	Country	Sport	Years	Medals
Michael Phelps	USA	swimming	2000–2016	28
Larisa Latynina	Soviet Union	gymnastics	1956–1964	18
Marit Bjoergen	Norway	cross-country skiing	2002–2018	15
Nikolai Andrianov	Soviet Union	gymnastics	1972–1980	15

Glossary

ancient (AYN-shunt)—from a long time ago

contestant (kuhn-TES-tuhnt)—a person who takes part in a competition

integrate (IN-tuh-grayt)—to open to people of all races

international tournament (in-tur-NASH-uh-nuhl TUR-nuh-muhnt)—a series of games between teams coming from different countries

modern (MOD-urn)—happening today or not long ago, compared to the distant past

Nazi (NOT-see)—National Socialist Party led by Adolf Hitler that controlled Germany before and during World War II (1939-1945)

podium (POH-dee-uhm)—the platform where the first-place, second-place, and third-place finishers stand after a contest to receive their medals

relay (REE-lay)—a race between teams in which each team member goes a certain distance and is then replaced by another team member

represent (rep-rih-ZENT)—to stand for something

white supremacy (WHITE soo-PREH-mah-see)—believing that the white race is superior to other races and that white people should have control over people of other races

Read More

International Olympic Committee. *The Story of the Olympic Games*. London: Welbeck Children's Books, 2021.

Motta, Veruska. *The Great Book of Olympic Games*. Milan, Italy: White Star, 2021.

Yomtov, Nel. *Defying Hitler: Jesse Owens' Olympic Triumph*. North Mankato, MN: Capstone, 2019.

Internet Sites

International Olympic Committee
olympics.com/en

National Geographic Kids: "Let the Games Begin: The First Olympics"
kids.nationalgeographic.com/history/article/first-olympics

Sports Illustrated Kids: "Olympics"
sikids.com/olympics

Index

1980 U.S. hockey team, 24–25

Barkley, Charles, 18
Biles, Simone, 6–7
Bolt, Usain, 10, 11
Brooks, Herb, 24

Comaneci, Nadia, 7

Dream Team, 18–19

Griffith-Joyner, Florence, 11

Heiden, Eric, 8–9
Henie, Sonja, 5
Hüfner, Tatjana, 11

Jingjing, Guo, 14
Jordan, Michael, 19
Joyner-Kersee, Jackie, 27

Kim, Chloe, 17
Kim, Yuna, 20–21

Lewis, Carl, 23, 29
Louganis, Greg, 14–15

Moir, Scott, 21

Owens, Jesse, 22–23

Phelps, Michael, 28–29

Rudolph, Wilma, 26–27

Virtue, Tessa, 21

White, Shaun, 16–17
Wickenheiser, Hayley, 24
Williams, Lauryn, 12–13
Wüst, Ireen, 8

About the Author

photo by Marta Berglund

Bruce Berglund is a writer and historian. For 19 years, he taught history at Calvin College and the University of Kansas. His courses included the history of China, Russia, women in Europe, sports, and war in modern society. He has earned three Fulbright awards and traveled to 17 countries for research and teaching. His most recent book is *The Fastest Game in the World*, a history of world hockey published by the University of California Press. Bruce works as a writer at Gustavus Adolphus College, and he teaches writing classes at the Loft Literary Center in Minneapolis. His four children grew up reading books from Capstone Press, especially the graphic novel versions of classic literature. Bruce grew up in Duluth and now lives in southern Minnesota.